Prayer made easy

Mark Water

HENDRICKSON
PUBLISHERS

Prayer Made Easy
Hendrickson Publishers, Inc.
P.O. Box 3473
Peabody, Massachusetts 01961-3473

Unless otherwise noted, Scripture
quotations are taken from HOLY
BIBLE, NEW INTERNATIONAL
VERSION copyright © 1973, 1978,
1984 by International Bible
Society. All rights reserved.

Photography supplied by Foxx
Photos, Goodshoot, Digital Vision
and Tony Cantale

Illustrations by
Tony Cantale Graphics

First printing — February 1999
Reprinted 1999, 2001

Manufactured in Hong Kong

Contents

Special pull-out chart

By way of introduction

Prayer is no optional extra

The Lord Jesus Christ taught that prayer is not something to do when we feel like it. Rather, it is a God-given responsibility.

Why pray?

Here are some good reasons

1. Jesus told his disciples to	"Then Jesus told his disciples a parable to show them that they should always pray and not give up."	*Luke 18:1*
2. Paul said Christians should	"Devote yourselves to prayer."	*Colossians 4:2*
3. God uses prayer to bless us	"Ask and it will be given to you."	*Matthew 7:7*
4. Jesus prayed	"He [Jesus] went into the hills to pray."	*Mark 6:46*

A key verse to help you in your praying

See how many ways this one verse teaches us about praying.

Ephesians 6:18	A one verse guide to prayer
"And pray in the Spirit ...	How to pray
... on all occasions ...	When to pray
... with all kinds of prayers ...	Using a variety of prayers
... and requests. ...	Asking is part of praying
... With this in mind, be alert ...	Praying is one way to be spiritually awake
... and always keep on praying ...	Persevere in prayer
... for all the saints.	Pray for fellow Christians.

How do I get started?

The secret of praying

The secret of praying is praying. There is no hidden technique called *How to pray*. The secret is just to pray. The disciples did not ask Jesus, "Teach us *how* to pray?" They asked, "Teach us to pray."

> "One day Jesus was praying in a certain place. When he finished, one of his disciples said to him, 'Lord, teach us to pray, just as John taught his disciples.'" *Luke 11:1*

Have you ever seen a prayer rock?

It is a small rock, wrapped in attractive fabric and tied with a ribbon. On the ribbon a card is attached, and on the card are the words: "My Prayer Rock," followed by this poem.

The prayer rock poem

I'm your little prayer rock and this is what I'd do.
Just put me on your pillow until the day is through.
Then turn back the covers and climb into your bed, and
"WHACK..." your little prayer rock will hit you
    on the head.
Then you will remember as the day is through,
to kneel and say your prayers as you wanted to.
Then when you are finished just dump me on the floor.
I'll stay there through the night to give you help once more.
When you get up in the morning "CLUNK,"
    I'll stub your toe,
So you will remember your morning prayers before you go.
Put me back upon your pillow when your bed is made.
Your clever little prayer rock will continue in your aid.
Because your heavenly Father cares and loves you so,
He wants you to remember to talk to him, you know!
Author unknown

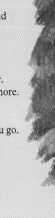

Use an alarm clock

Many Christians find that the morning is the best time to pray. For some people the most important thing in their prayer life is an alarm clock.

If you don't get up in time to have an unhurried period of prayer, don't be surprised that you skip prayer throughout the day. Hence the need for an alarm clock.

> "Very early in the morning, while it was
> still dark, Jesus got up, left the house
> and went off to a solitary place,
> where he prayed."
> *Mark 1:35*

A. C. T. S.

So, you've made it!

You've actually got up in time
to pray. Well done! That's more
than some Christians ever manage to do!

What do you do now? These next ten pages give a simple
outline you may wish to follow. If you do, you will cover some
of the most important areas of prayer.

A. C. T. S.

A. C. T. S. stands for the Acts of the Apostles, with each letter
representing a different aspect of prayer.

A = Adoration (or worshiping God)
C = Confession of sins to God
T = Thanksgiving
S = Supplication, asking for things in prayer

Think about whom you are praying to

Try and lose yourself in prayer, as you focus on God.
This is how the writer to the Hebrews advises us to approach
God.

"Therefore, since we have a great
high priest who has gone through
the heavens, Jesus the Son of
God, let us hold firmly to the faith
we profess. For we do not have a
high priest who is unable to
sympathize with our weaknesses,
but we have one who has been
tempted in every way, just as we
are – yet was without sin. Let us
then approach the throne of grace
with confidence, so that we may
receive mercy and find grace to
help us in our time of need."
Hebrews 4:14-16

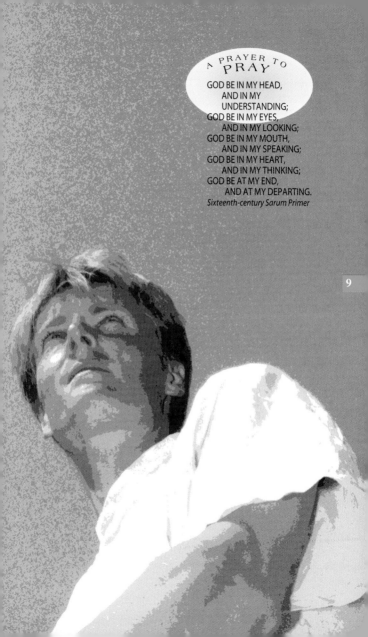

A PRAYER TO PRAY

GOD BE IN MY HEAD,
    AND IN MY
        UNDERSTANDING;
GOD BE IN MY EYES,
    AND IN MY LOOKING;
GOD BE IN MY MOUTH,
    AND IN MY SPEAKING;
GOD BE IN MY HEART,
    AND IN MY THINKING;
GOD BE AT MY END,
    AND AT MY DEPARTING.

Sixteenth-century Sarum Primer

A is for adoration

Adoration
This is a time to remember who God is.
Praise him:
> for his love,
> his power,
> his majesty,
> > and for his wonderful gift of Jesus.

A SAYING ABOUT
PRAYER
"WHEN WE BECOME TOO GLIB
IN PRAYER WE ARE MOST SURELY
TALKING TO OURSELVES."
A.W. Tozer

Hum a hymn
You may like to sing a chorus like *Majesty* or a traditional hymn like *How Great Thou Art* or *A Mighty Fortress is Our God*.

This will help you to worship God as you start your time of prayer. It helps you to remember God's greatness and your own dependence on him.

Music
You may try playing a track of Christian music from a CD or cassette.

Using a hymn book
At the beginning of your time of prayer, try praying one hymn a day from the Praise or Worship section of a hymn book.

Some psalms of worship
Turn to a psalm to help your spirit as a means to start praising God. Try one of these each day, for a month.

Psalm number
19; 29; 33; 34; 35; 47; 50; 76; 87; 91; 93;
95; 96; 99; 100; 104; 107; 111; 113; 114; 115; 117;
121; 134; 139; 145; 146; 147; 148; 150.

> **Psalm 117**
> "Praise the Lord, all you nations;
>   extol him, all you peoples.
> For great is his love towards us,
>   and the faithfulness of the Lord endures for ever.
> Praise the Lord."
> *Psalm 117:1-2*

An acrostic on P-R-A-Y-E-R

Prayer is made up of:

P<small>ETITION</small>:	"He [Daniel] still prays three times a day."	*Daniel 6:13*
R<small>EVERENCE</small>:	"Worship God acceptably with reverence and awe."	*Hebrews 12:28*
A<small>DORATION</small>:	"My lips will glorify you."	*Psalm 63:3*
Y<small>EARNING</small>:	"Blessed are those who hunger and thirst after righteousness."	*Matthew 5:6*
E<small>XPECTATION</small>:	"Elijah ... prayed earnestly that it might not rain."	*James 5:17*
R<small>EQUESTS</small>:	"Present your requests to God."	*Philippians 4:6*

C is for confessing sin

Confessing sin to God

It's not as if you are telling God anything he does not already know when you admit to him your sins. But it does show that you
are sorry for them and that you really do want his forgiveness and are determined (with his help) not to keep on repeating the same old sins, day after day.

This time of owning up to your sin is a time to be honest and humble.

God never stops loving you, no matter how sinful you have been. Be reassured about this. Read Luke 15:11-32 and focus on the love of the father in this story of the prodigal son.

Remember: God loves you like that.

A SAYING ABOUT **PRAYER**
"MORE THINGS ARE WROUGHT BY PRAYER THAN THIS WORLD DREAMS OF."
Lord Alfred Tennyson

Peter's advice, quoting Psalm 34

"For the eyes of the Lord are on the righteous
and his ears are attentive to their prayer,
but the face of the Lord is against those who do evil."
1 Peter 3:12

There is only one way to be righteous in God's sight,
and that is to confess our sin to him and to accept as a gift
the righteousness of Jesus.

God's assures us that he will forgive us

"If we claim to be without sin, we deceive ourselves and the truth is not in us. If we confess our sins, he [God] is faithful and just and will forgive us our sins and purify us from all unrighteousness."
1 John 1:9

Confess your sin before you pray for others

The order in which you pray is not important. We move constantly between adoration, confession, thanksgiving and supplication. But if we want God to hear and answer our prayers we need to confess and let go of our own sin.

A wonderful promise

Buried deep in the Old Testament is this wonderful promise that if we confess our sin to God he will listen to and answer our prayers.

> "If my people, who are called by
>   my name,
> will humble themselves
> and pray
> and seek my face
> and *turn from their wicked ways*,
> then I will hear them from
>   heaven and will forgive their
>   sin and will heal their land."
> *2 Chronicles 7:14*

A PRAYER TO PRAY

THE JESUS PRAYER
LORD JESUS CHRIST, SON OF GOD,
HAVE MERCY ON ME, A SINNER.
*For many centuries Eastern Orthodox
Christians have used this prayer as a basis
for their praying and daily living.*

T is for thanksgiving

Thanksgiving
Before you start thinking about what you are going to pray for, spend some moments in giving thanks to God.

"Give thanks in all circumstances."
1 Thessalonians 5:18

"Give thanks to the Lord ... remember the wonders he has done." *Psalm 104:1,5*

Thank God for his forgiveness
Praise the Lord, O my soul,
    and forget not all his benefits –
who forgives all your sins
    and heals all your diseases, ...
For as high as the heavens are above the earth,
    so great is his love for those who fear him;
as far as the east is from the west,
    so far has he removed our transgressions from us.
Psalm 103:2-3, 11-12

Why and when we are to give thanks to God

1. As we approach him.	"Let us come before him with thanksgiving."	*Psalm 95:2*
2. For the gift of Jesus.	"Thanks be to God for his indescribable gift!"	*2 Corinthians 9:15*
3. Because God is good.	"Give thanks to the Lord, for he is good."	*Psalm 136:1*
4. For deliverance from sin's grip.	"I see ... the law of sin at work within my members. What a wretched man I am! Who will rescue me from this body of death? Thanks be to God – through Jesus Christ our Lord!	*Romans 7:23-25*
5. All of God's good gifts.	"For everything God created is good, and nothing is to be rejected if it is received with thanksgiving, because it is consecrated by the word of God and prayer."	*1 Timothy 4:4-5*
6. The defeat of death and sin.	"But thanks be to God! He gives us the victory through our Lord Jesus Christ."	*1 Corinthians 15:57*
7. Give thanks continually.	"Through Jesus, therefore, let us continually offer to God a sacrifice of praise."	*Hebrews 13:15*

Only one in ten bothered to say "thank you"

Jesus healed ten lepers, see Luke 17:11-19, but only one went back to Jesus to thank him.

"One of them, when he saw he was healed, came back, praising God in a loud voice. He threw himself at Jesus' feet and thanked him – and he was a Samaritan."
Luke 17:16

S is for supplication

Supplication

This is the time to make specific requests in prayer, both for
others and for yourself.

Four prayer topics from the Bible	
1. The sick	*James 5:14-16*
2. Rulers	*1 Timothy 2:1-3*
3. More Christian workers	"Jesus went through all the towns and villages, teaching in their synagogues, preaching the good news of the kingdom and healing every disease and sickness. When he saw the crowds, he had compassion on them, because they were harassed and helpless, like sheep without a shepherd. Then he said to his disciples, 'The harvest is plentiful but the workers are few. Ask the Lord of the harvest, therefore, to send out workers into his harvest field.'" *Matthew 9:35-38*
4. Yourself	*1 Chronicles 4:10; Psalm 106:4-5*

David Brainerd

The Life and Diary of David Brainerd, published after his death by his friend Jonathan Edwards, has probably influenced more revivals than any other book. His life was one of burning prayer for the American Indians. Brainerd was converted at the age of twenty-one and immediately became a pioneer missionary. He spent six years of astonishing, agonizing prayer until, in 1744, when he was twenty-seven, a remarkable revival swept over his work.

Brainerd's Journal

The following extract from Brainerd's journal was written in 1742, when he had been a Christian for three years and was twenty-four years old.

"I set apart this day for secret fasting and prayer, to entreat God to direct and bless me with regard to the great work I have in view, of preaching the gospel. Just last night the Lord visited me marvelously in prayer: I think my soul never was in such an agony before. I felt no restraint; for the treasures of divine grace were opened before me.

I wrestled for absent friends, for the ingathering of souls, and for the children of God in many distant places. I was in such agony, from sun half an hour high, till near dark, that I was all over wet with sweat. Oh, my dear Jesus did sweat blood for poor souls! I longed for more compassion towards them."

Pray through your day

Go through your day in prayer asking for God's special help over the worrisome things or anything that you are dreading.

A SAYING ABOUT
PRAYER

TALKING TO PEOPLE ABOUT GOD IS A GREAT PRIVILEGE, BUT TALKING TO GOD FOR PEOPLE IS GREATER STILL.

Does God always answer our requests?

God always gives an answer – but sometimes it may be "no," or "wait," or "I have a better way." This is what Paul found out. *See 2 Corinthians 12:9-10*

Where and to whom should I pray?

Who am I praying to?

Many people think of God as:

- a distant tyrant
- a sort of slot-machine
- an impersonal force

When we pray we are talking to a good and loving Father – the sort of Father all our fathers ought to copy.

Loving Father

1. A loving Father	"Which of you fathers, if your son asks for a fish, will give him a snake instead? Or if he asks for an egg, will give him a scorpion?"	*Luke 11:11*
	"If you, then, though you are evil, know how to give good gifts to your children, how much more will your Father in heaven give good gifts to those who ask him!"	*Matthew 7:11*
2. Your Father	"To all who received him ... he gave the right to become children of God."	*John 1:12*

Where to pray

1. In private	"But when your pray, go into your room, close the door and pray to your Father, who is unseen."	*Matthew 6:6*
2. In public	"So they took away the stone. [Just before the raising of Lazarus.] Jesus looked up and said, 'Father, I thank you that you have heard me. I knew that your always hear me, but I said this for the benefit of the people standing here, that they may believe that you send me."	*John 11:42*
3. Anywhere	"Pray continually."	*1 Thessalonians 5:17*

Wherever you are

1. As you wake	Let your waking thoughts turn to thank God for his goodness and for a new day. "When I awake I am still with you."	*Psalm 139:18*
2. As you wash and dress	As you wash let the running water be a symbol of God's cleansing and his refreshment of your soul. As you dress say over in your mind or aloud a phrase from a Bible verse you know. Or, think about one of Jesus' kind actions recorded in the Gospels.	
3. In the middle of the day	Snatch a moment to be quiet in your mind. Recall a promise of Jesus, like, "I am with you always."	*Matthew 28:20*
4. As you go to sleep	Make a promise to God as you lay on your pillow to rest. "I will lie down and sleep in peace, for you alone, O Lord, make me dwell in safety."	*Psalm 4:8*
5. If you are wakeful	Try repeating over and over again a Bible verse or part of a verse, about God's comfort. "The Lord is my shepherd, I shall not be in want."	*Psalm 23:1*

When and how and what should I pray?

Set times for prayer

There's no one rule about this. Many Christians like to pray first thing in the morning and last thing at night.

A SAYING ABOUT *PRAYER*

YOU WILL NEVER BE ABLE TO PRAY EVERYWHERE, ALL THE TIME, UNTIL YOU HAVE LEARNED TO PRAY SOMEWHERE, SOME OF THE TIME.

In addition, some people try to follow the practice of short periods of prayer at 6 AM, 9 AM, 12 noon, 3 PM, 6 PM, 9 PM, and 12 midnight.

"Seven times a day I praise you." *Psalm 119:164*

Should I kneel when I pray?

You can kneel, sit, stand, or raise your hands. It really doesn't matter. Prayer is meant to be a time when we express our dependence on God. Many Christians find that kneeling helps them to do this.

How did people pray in the Bible?

1. They often knelt	"Come let us bow down in worship, let us kneel before the Lord our Maker."	*Psalm 95:6*
	"Every knee will bow before me; every tongue will confess to God."	*Romans 14:11*
	"... and there on the beach we knelt to pray."	*Acts 21:5*
2. They lifted up their hands	"Lift up your hands in the sanctuary and praise the Lord."	*Psalm 134:2*
	"I will praise you as long as I live, and in your name I will lift up my hands."	*Psalm 63:4*
	"I urge, then, first of all, that requests, prayers, intercession and thanksgiving be made for everyone ... I want men everywhere to lift up holy hands in prayer."	*1 Timothy 2:1,8*

What should I pray for?

If you want to pray for the same kinds of things that the early Christians prayed for, go through a New Testament letter and see what the writer prayed for and what he asked prayer for.

10 Prayer topics in the Acts of the Apostles

Topic	Reference in Acts
1. Prayer for unity	1:14
2. Prayer to know God's will	1:24
3. Prayer in church services	3:1
4. Prayer linked to preaching	6:4
5. Prayer for new Christians	8:15
6. Prayer for persecuted Christians	12:5
7. Prayer for missionaries	13:2-4
8. Prayer when in severe trouble	16:25
9. Prayer for Christian leaders	21:5
10. Prayer for healing	28:8

Praying on your own

Praying in the Spirit

All true prayer is praying in the Spirit.

For you either pray just using your own efforts or else you pray in the Spirit, with the help of the Holy Spirit.

> "But you, dear friends, build yourselves up in your most holy faith and pray in the Holy Spirit." *Jude 20*

> "And pray in the Spirit ..." *Ephesians 6:18*

A book of prayers

Try praying one prayer a day from a book of traditional or contemporary prayers.

Coping with distractions

For some people, like mothers with toddlers, there is hardly five minutes of calm and quiet in the day or even through the night!

Don't worry if you're unable to have a long time of quiet for prayer. You can still pray short prayers (sometimes called *sentence prayers*) to God through your day. Remember: Jesus understands. He grew up in a large family. He had at least four younger half-brothers and at least two younger half-sisters.

> "Isn't this the carpenter? Isn't this Mary's son and the brother of James, Joseph, Judas and Simon? Aren't his sisters here with us?" *Mark 6:3*

But even without the demands of a family, some people find that their thoughts begin to wander as soon as they start to pray. If you find that you start to think about things you had forgotten, keep a pencil and paper at hand to write these things down. Then you can forget them until you have finished praying.

Are my prayers being heard?

Most Christians have wondered about this. We have Jesus's promises to rest on – nothing more and nothing less.

> "Until now you have not asked for anything in my name. Ask and you will receive, and your joy will be complete."
> *John 16:24*

Spiritual warfare

Remember: prayer is a great spiritual battle. The last thing in the world Satan wants you to be able to do is to have a time when you pray to God.

Jesus is interested in you and your needs

Think positively. The Lord Jesus Christ is your Savior and Friend. So you have the unique privilege of speaking directly with your heavenly Father through him.

Paul says to pray like this:

> "Do not be anxious about anything, but in everything, by prayer and petition, with thanksgiving, present your requests to God."
> *Philippians 4:6*

A PRAYER TO PRAY

O LORD, YOU KNOW HOW BUSY I MUST BE THIS DAY. IF I FORGET YOU, DO NOT FORGET ME.
General Lord Astley (1579-1652) before the battle of Edgehill

Praying in a small group

The Acts 2:42 model

The first Christians did not just pray as isolated individuals – they encouraged each other as they prayed together.

Acts 2:42	Lessons to learn
"They devoted themselves ...	They took their spiritual life very seriously
... to the apostles' teaching ...	They wanted to build up their faith with teaching.
... and to the fellowship ...	They kept in close contact with fellow Christians.
... to the breaking of the bread ...	They remembered Jesus' death and resurrection
... and to prayer."	Prayer was essential to them.

Prayer partners

Some churches and college fellowships encourage people to pray with one or two other Christians. In two's they are called prayer partners; in three's they are called prayer triplets, etc.

Seek out a small prayer group or a be a third of a prayer triplet!

A word of warning

It's easy to operate independently and free of restraints in small groups where no one can read your mind or see your heart.

To talk spiritually is one thing – to be spiritual is something altogether different. You need to be just as spiritually alert in a small group as in a large congregation. Jesus warned against such hypocrisy:

> "These people honor me with their lips but their hearts are far from me." *Matthew 15:8*

The way to stop yourself from being careless about prayer, either on your own or with other people, is to ask God to keep you humble.

> "This is the one I esteem:
> he who is humble and contrite in spirit,
> and trembles at my word."
> *Isaiah 66:2*

The Bible and prayer

Praying and reading the Bible should always be linked. You should pray before, during and after you read the Bible. You should expect God to speak to you as you read, and then pray about what he has said.

Our experience at these times should be like that of the two disciples who walked to Emmaus with the risen Lord Jesus.

> "Were not our hearts burning within us while he talked with us on the road and opened the Scriptures to us?" *Luke 24:32*

For how long should I pray?

There is no set time length to aim at

It's best to start small. Try setting aside five minutes a day. It's better to manage a short time of prayer than to be continually failing to pray for a longer period.

After a while you will doubtless find that you *want* to pray for longer than five minutes a day.

All night?

"One of those days Jesus went out to a mountainside to pray, and spent the night praying to God." *Luke 6:12*

This was unusual. It was also for a specific reason.

"When morning came, he called his disciples to him and chose twelve of them." *Luke 6:13*

Persistence in prayer

On many occasions Jesus taught that his followers should persist in prayer.

"Ask and it will be given to you; seek and you will find; knock and the door will be opened to you. For everyone who asks receives; he who seeks finds; and to him who knocks, the door will be opened." *Matthew 7:7-8*

"AND WHEN YOU PRAY, DO NOT KEEP ON BABBLING LIKE THE PAGANS, FOR THEY THINK THEY WILL BE HEARD FOR THEIR MANY WORDS."
Matthew 6:7

He waited for twenty years

There was one man in the Old Testament who had to wait twenty years for his prayer to be answered.

"This is the account of Abraham's son Isaac. Abraham became the father of Isaac, and Isaac was forty years old when he married Rebekah daughter of Bethuel the Aramean from Paddan Aram and sister of Laban the Aramean. Isaac prayed to the Lord on behalf of his wife, because she was barren. The Lord answered his prayer, and his wife Rebekah became pregnant. ... Isaac was sixty years old when Rebekah gave birth." *Genesis 25:19-21, 26*

Points to note
1. Isaac was forty when he was married.
2. Rebekah was barren.
3. Isaac was sixty when Rebekah became pregnant.

A PRAYER TO PRAY

O MOST MERCIFUL REDEEMER,
FRIEND AND BROTHER,
MAY WE KNOW YOU MORE CLEARLY,
LOVE YOU MORE DEARLY,
AND FOLLOW YOU MORE NEARLY,
DAY BY DAY.
Richard of Chichester

The Jesus prayer

The disciple's prayer

The Lord's prayer has been given many names: *The Lord's Prayer; The Jesus Prayer; The Our Father; Pater Noster* (the first two words in Latin, translating "Our Father"); *The Christian's Model Prayer*. It has also been called *The Disciple's Prayer*.

When we pray the Lord's Prayer, we come:

1. As God's children	*Our Father*
2. As worshipers	*Hallowed be your name*
3. As subject	*Your kingdom come*
4. As servants	*Your will be done*
5. As recipients	*Give us this day our daily bread*
6. As sinners	*Forgive us our sins*
7. As tempted ones	*Lead us not into temptation*
8. As victorious people	*But deliver us from the evil one*

Try praying through the Lord's Prayer, slowly, taking up to a minute per petition, remembering all the different "people" you are.

I cannot say

I cannot say "our" if I live only for myself.

I cannot say "Father" if I do not endeavor each day to act like his child.

I cannot say "in heaven" if I am laying up no treasure there.

I cannot say "hallowed be your name" if I am not striving for holiness.

I cannot say "your kingdom come" if I am not doing all in my power to hasten that wonderful event.

I cannot say "your will be done" if I am disobedient to his word.

I cannot say "on earth as it is in heaven" if I'll not serve him here and now.

I cannot say "give us today our daily bread" if I am dishonest or seeking things by subterfuge.

I cannot say "forgive us our debts" if I harbor a grudge against anyone.

I cannot say "lead us not into temptation" if I deliberately place myself in its path.

I cannot say "deliver us from evil" if I do not put on the whole armor of God.

I cannot say "yours is the kingdom" if I do not give the King the loyalty due him from a faithful subject.

I cannot attribute to him "the power" if I fear what men may do.

I cannot ascribe to him "the glory" if I'm seeking honor only for myself.

And I cannot say "for ever" if the horizon of my life is bounded completely by time.

Author unknown

29

Our Father in heaven

A heavenly Father
God the Father is our heavenly Father and he cares for us.

"Therefore I tell you, do not worry about your life, what you will eat or drink; or about your body, what you will wear. Is not life more important than food, and the body more important than clothes?

"Look at the birds of the air; they do not sow or reap or store away in barns, and yet your heavenly Father feeds them. Are you not much more valuable than they?

"Who of you by worrying can add a single hour to his life?"
Matthew 6:25-28

A SAYING ABOUT
PRAYER
"IN PRAYER IT IS BETTER TO HAVE
A HEART WITHOUT WORDS THAN
WORDS WITHOUT A HEART."
John Bunyan

Father
The Greek word Jesus uses for "Father" in the Lord's Prayer is *pater*.

When Jesus prayed to his Father in the Garden of Gethsemane he used another word for Father, as well as *pater*. It was the Aramaic word *Abba*. So he prayed, *"Abba, pater."*

"'*Abba*, Father,' he said, 'everything is possible for you.'"
Mark 14:36

Abba
When we are born again we are adopted into God's family and God became our spiritual Father. As the apostle Paul put it, "Because you are sons, God sent the Spirit of his Son into our hearts, the Spirit who calls out 'Abba, Father'."
Galatians 4:6

As Jesus prayed, *"Abba, pater,"* so we are to pray, *"Abba, pater."*

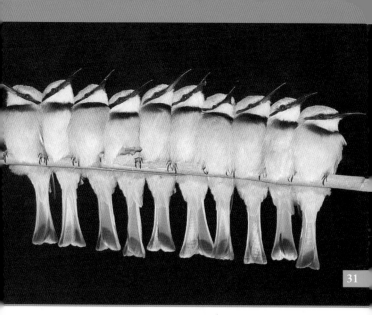

Our Father in heaven

It is not possible to translate the word *Abba* into English. Many of the Bible translations keep the word *Abba* and don't attempt any translation. At the time of Jesus it was the word a toddler called his father. Today Arab children called their father *jaba*. *Abba* is the Eastern word for Daddy.

Jesus was now telling his disciples that when they start praying they come to the God of heaven, who is so close to them that they have the privilege of praying "*our* Father in heaven."

Look at the birds of the air

Said the Robin to the Sparrow:
    "I should really like to know,
Why these anxious human beings
    Rush around and worry so?"

Said the Sparrow to the Robin:
    "Friend, I think it must be,
That they have no heavenly Father
    Such as cares for you and me!"

Hallowed be your name

Praying in the name of Jesus

Prayer must be in the name of Jesus Christ.

> "I will do whatever you ask in my name." *John 14:13*

In biblical times someone's name indicated their nature, who they were. So when we pray "in Jesus' name" we are identifying ourselves with him, having accepted his salvation.

What's in a name?

The Lord is so great that the Bible uses many different names for God to help us appreciate different aspects of his amazing nature. People have found it helpful to meditate on God's nature as revealed in adjectives associated with his name in Hebrew.

The name of the Lord

> "The name of the Lord is a strong tower, the righteous run to it and are safe."

Names linked to God

Hebrew name	English name	Bible verses to look up
1. *Shalom*	Peace, rest, contentment	*Isaiah 53:5; Hebrews 4:9-10; John 14:27; Philippians 4:7; Colossians 1:19-20* "He called it The Lord is Peace." *Judges 6:24*
2. *Zidkenu*	Righteousness, perfection	*Jeremiah 23:6; 2 Corinthians 5:21; 1 Corinthians 1:30* "For in the gospel a righteousness from God is revealed." *Romans 1:17*
3. *M'kaddesh*	Sanctifies, purifies	*Isaiah 6; 1 Corinthians 6:9-11; Romans 8:29* "May God himself ... sanctify you through and through." *1 Thessalonians 5:23*
4. *Rophe*	Heals	*Exodus 15:26.* "By his wounds you have been healed." *1 Peter 2:24*
5. *Yira*	Who sees, provides	*Psalm 34:15,18* "So Abraham called that place The Lord Will Provide." *Genesis 22:14*
6. *Nissi*	Banner, security, captain	*1 Corinthians 15:56-57* "Moses built an altar and called it The Lord is my Banner." *Exodus 17:15*
7. *Rohi*	Shepherd, companion, friend	*Proverbs 18:24; 1 Peter 2:25* "The Lord is my shepherd." *Psalm 23:1*

Hallowed

As you praise your Father God for who he is you begin to worship him, to adore God, to hallow his name.

"Ascribe to the Lord the glory due unto His name ... Worship the Lord in the splendor of his holiness." *1 Chronicles 16:29*

Two kinds of praise and adoration

As you pray praise God for who he is and for what he has done.

"Enter his gates with thanksgiving and his courts with praise; give thanks to him and praise his name." *Psalm 100:4*

Your kingdom come

Two thoughts about God's kingdom

God's "kingdom" means God's rule.

1. It is within Christians.	"The kingdom of God is within you."	*Luke 17:21*
2. It has priority over everything else.	"But first seek his kingdom and his righteousness, and all these things will be given to you as well.	*Matthew 6:33*

A SAYING ABOUT
PRAYER

"THY WILL BE DONE,
BY ME NOW!"
C.S. Lewis

Praying for God's kingdom to come

1. For God's worldwide church

"Your kingdom come" has been called the greatest missionary prayer ever prayed. It includes the whole world as we ask that God's rule should be extended to every part of the globe.

2. For a church fellowship

"Your kingdom come" is the best prayer to pray for any church. This is how Paul prayed for the Ephesian church.

Ephesians 1:15-19	Prayer topics & points to note
Verse 15: "For this reason, ever since I heard about your faith in the Lord Jesus and your love for all the saints,	1. People becoming Christians 2. Their love for fellow Christians
Verse 16: I have not stopped giving thanks for you, remembering you in prayers.	3. Paul's constant praying and the emphasis on giving thanks.
Verse 17: I keep asking that the God of our Lord Jesus Christ, the glorious Father, may give you the Spirit of wisdom and revelation, so that you may know him better.	4. The Spirit of wisdom 5. The Spirit of revelation 6. To know Jesus better
Verse 18: I pray also that the eyes of your heart may be enlightened in order that you may know the hope to which he has called you, the riches of his glorious inheritance in the saints,	7. Inner enlightenment 8. To know our future hope 9. To enjoy God's inheritance
Verse 19: and his incomparably great power for us who believe.	10. To know God's great power

3. In our own lives

There is little point in praying for God's kingdom to be strengthened everywhere in the world if we do not want God to be King in our own lives.

The prayer we need to pray for ourselves should be along the lines of Paul's advice to the Christians at Rome.

"Therefore, I urge you, brothers, in view of God's mercy, to offer your bodies as living sacrifices, holy and pleasing to God – this is your spiritual act of worship." *Romans 12:1*

Your will be done on earth as it is in heaven

The place of God's will in our lives

1. God's will is to have priority over our will	"Yet not as I will, but as you will... May your will be done."	*Matthew 26:39,42*
2. Jesus' overriding desire was to do God's will.	"'My food'", said Jesus, 'is to do the will of him who sent me.'"	*John 4:34*
3. We are expected to find out what God's will is.	"Find out what pleases the Lord ... understand what the Lord's will is."	*Ephesians 5:10,17*

Praying "your will be done" for your own life

Paul reminded the Christians at Rome that God's will would only be carried out in their lives if they submitted their minds to God's will and God's renewal.

A SAYING ABOUT PRAYER

IF YOU ARE TOO BUSY TO PRAY, THEN YOU ARE TOO BUSY.

> "Do not be conformed to this world, but be transformed by the renewing of your minds, so that you may discern what is the will of God –
> what is good
> and acceptable
> and perfect."
> *Romans 12:2*

A PRAYER TO PRAY

O LORD, MAKE YOUR WAY PLAIN BEFORE ME.
LET YOUR GLORY BE MY END,
YOUR WORD MY RULE,
AND THEN YOUR WILL BE DONE.
AMEN.

King Charles I (1600-1649)

Praying for God's will

Pray for God's will to be done
in your family
in your church
in your relationships
in your city
in your nation
and in the world.

Give us today our daily bread

A prayer of dependence

When we pray, "Give us today our daily bread," we are expressing our dependence on God for all our needs, both spiritual and material.

A good daily prayer comes in Proverbs:

> "Keep falsehood and lies far from me; give me neither poverty or riches, but give me only my daily bread." *Proverbs 30:8*

A prayer for daily needs

It is a natural human reaction to difficulties to be anxious about not having what we need. This part of the Lord's prayer stresses "prayer and supplication with thanksgiving," as the Christian reaction to trouble.

> "Do not be anxious about anything, but by prayer and supplication with thanksgiving let your requests be made known to God, and the peace of God, which surpasses all understanding, will guard your hearts and your minds in Christ Jesus." *Philippians 4:6-7*

Daily bread and daily worry

The question is: If we believe that God is our loving heavenly Father, why do we worry so much?

Look at the birds

"Therefore I tell you, do not worry about your life, what you will eat or drink; or about your body, what you will wear. Is not life more important than food, and the body more important than clothes? Look at the birds of the air; they do not sow or reap or store away in barns, and yet your heavenly Father feeds them. Are you not much more valuable than they? Who of you by worrying can add a single hour to his life?" *Matthew 6:25-27*

Give *us* our daily bread

We find it easier to pray for our own daily needs than for those of the hungry and starving. Now that we live in a global village and know the plight of needy people in many different parts of the world, we can see very clearly that this part of the Lord's Prayer should extend to the whole world.

A seemingly kind word, but no action

James warned his readers about the gap between kind ideas and positive action for the needy.

> "Suppose a brother or sister is without clothes and daily food. If one of you says to him, 'Go, I wish you well; keep warm and well fed,' but does nothing about his physical needs, what good is it?"
> *James 2:15-16*

Forgive us ...
as we also have forgiven

No automatic forgiveness

The is the only part of the Lord's Prayer which Jesus
immediately went on to explain.

> "For if you forgive men when they sin against you, your heavenly
> Father will also forgive you. But if you do not forgive men their sins,
> your Father will not forgive your sins." *Matthew 6:14-15*

Forgive others

We have our sins forgiven by our loving heavenly Father. He
expects us to be kind and forgiving towards others.

> "Be kind and compassionate to one another,
> forgiving each other, just as in Christ God
> forgave you." *Ephesians 4:32*

Removing the sin barrier

For some people, forgiving other people
seems an impossible height to climb
and God's special help needs to
be asked.

   Holding a grudge against
someone is a sin. Any
unconfessed sin and any sin
we don't want to root out
from our lives has a very
serious consequence on
our praying.

> "But your iniquities have
> separated you from your God;
> your sins have hidden his face
> from you, so that he will not
> hear you." *Isaiah 59:2*

Time for a spiritual check up

Praying this part of the Lord's Prayer gives you an opportunity to give yourself a spiritual check up.

• Ask the Holy Spirit to show you your sins.

Pray this prayer from the psalms.

"Search me, O God, and know my heart; test me and know my anxious thoughts. See if there is any offensive way in me, and lead me in the way everlasting." *Psalm 139:23-24*

• Confess your sins to God, being as specific as possible.

Recall this proverb.

"He who conceals his sins does not prosper, but whoever confesses and renounces them finds mercy." *Proverbs 28:13*

• Make restitution or amends as necessary.

What did Jesus say on this subject? Jesus said we are to put things right with other people before we worship him.

"Therefore, if you are offering your gift at the altar and there remember that your brother has something against you, leave your gift there in front of the altar. First go and be reconciled to your brother; then come and offer your gift." *Matthew 5:23-24*

41

A PRAYER TO PRAY

FATHER, SEEING HOW FREELY YOU HAVE LOVED ME WITH MY IMPERFECTIONS, GRANT THAT I MAY EQUALLY LOVE OTHERS WITH THEIRS. AMEN.
Author unknown

Lead us not into temptation

Being tempted is no sin in itself

Jesus was himself tempted on many occasions. It is giving way to temptation that is sinful.

> "Then Jesus was led by the Spirit into the desert to be tempted by the devil." *Matthew 4:1*

An analysis of temptation

1 Corinthians 10:13	Lessons to learn
"No temptation has seized you except what is common to man."	**1.** Everyone is tempted. Yes everyone from the Christian you admire the most, down to yourself. No one escapes temptation.
"And God is faithful."	**2.** God is not letting us down by allowing a temptation to attack us. He promises to stay at our side through it.
"He will not let you be tempted beyond what you can bear."	**3.** God knows our limits. He promises that we will never be tempted beyond the power he gives us.
"But when you are tempted, he will also provide a way out so that you can stand up under it."	**4.** We need to turn to God in prayer before, during and after temptation. He promises to help us and to provide a way out of temptation so we must go to him for this supernatural assistance.

Overcoming temptation

Some Christians claim that, in answer to prayer, God has instantly and miraculously delivered them from a particular temptation. But the experience of most Christians is that the battle against temptation is life-long. God has provided a number of spiritual weapons for Christians to use in this spiritual warfare.

• The Bible

When faced with temptation, Jesus quoted the Bible against the Tempter. *See Matthew 4:4, 7, 11*

Using memorized Bible verses can be a great help when you are being tempted.

"I have hidden your word in my heart that I might not sin against you." *Psalm 119:11*

• Humility

It is when we think that we are doing fine and won't fall under temptation that we are most at risk of falling.

"So, if you think you are standing firm, be careful that you don't fall!" *1 Corinthians 10:12*

• Watchfulness and prayerfulness

At one of the most critical moments in Jesus' life (in the Garden of Gethsemane) Jesus told his disciples to watch and pray.

"*Watch and pray* so that you will not fall into temptation." *Matthew 26:41*

Recording the same event Luke writes that Jesus said: "Pray so that you will not fall into temptation." *Luke 22:40*

Deliver us from the evil one

The devil tempts, God tests
The devil tempts us in order to knock us down; God tests us in order to build us up.

> "When tempted, no one should say, 'God is tempting me.' For God cannot be tempted by evil, nor does he tempt anyone." *James 1:13*

A spiritual battle
Followers of Jesus face a spiritual battle every day. Satan wants to defeat us through temptation. So we pray for God's protection as we pray the Lord's Prayer.

Francis of Assisi
Francis of Assisi suggested that we should pray the following prayer when we come to this part of the Lord's Prayer.

> "Protect us from past evil.
> Protect us from present evil.
> Free us from future evil."

Handy hint from James
James told his readers how to defeat the devil. We do what he says as we pray this last part of the Lord's Prayer.

> "Submit yourselves, then, to God. Resist the devil, and he will flee from you." *James 4:7*

The kingdom, the power, and the glory

At the end of the Lord's Prayer we often pray what is known as the doxology, "For yours is the kingdom, and the power and the glory, for ever and ever. Amen."

These words may have been added by a scribe and may not have been given by Jesus in his original prayer. Yet they are suitable words to round off the Lord Prayer as the words – kingdom, power and glory – are strongly featured in the Bible.

• God's power

"Be strong in the Lord and in his mighty power."
Ephesians 6:10

• God's kingdom

"All you have made will praise you, O Lord; your saints will extol you. They will tell of the glory of your kingdom and speak of your might, so that all men may know of your mighty acts and the glorious splendor of your kingdom. Your kingdom is an everlasting kingdom, and your dominion endures through all generations."
Psalm 145:10-13

• God's glory

"Yours, O Lord, is the greatness and the power and the glory and the majesty and the splendor, for everything in heaven and earth is yours. Yours, O Lord, is the kingdom; you are exalted as head over all." *1 Chronicles 29:11*

Psalms for times of crisis

Prayer book and hymn book

In Old Testament times the Psalms were the prayer book and hymn book of God's people. Jews and Christians alike have drawn strength from them.

The one hundred and fifty psalms cover a wide variety of themes and it is helpful to know which psalms suit our particular needs.

Psalms in a time of crisis

1. Choose a psalm to read.
2. Read it all the way through.
3. Ask God to comfort you through its words.
4. Read it again, verse by verse. Pause and reflect on each verse before moving on to the next one.

Psalm 23

Psalm 23 has been called the Shepherd's Psalm. But the shepherd does not speak at all. So it has also been called the Sheep's Psalm, for the sheep do all the speaking.

The Lord is my shepherd, I shall not be in want.
He makes me lie down in green pastures,
he leads me beside quiet waters,
    he restores my soul.
He guides me in paths of righteousness
    for his name's sake.
Even though I walk
    through the valley of the shadow of death,
I will fear no evil,
    for you are with me;
your rod and your staff,
    they comfort me.
Your prepare a table before me
    in the presence of my enemies.
You anoint my head with oil;
    my cup overflows.
Surely goodness and love will follow me
    all the days of my life,
and I will dwell in the house of the Lord
    for ever.
Psalm 23:1-6

You prepare a table before me

This "table" was essential to wounded or sick sheep.

Healthy sheep did not care for ill sheep. At best, they would go over to the sick sheep and eat all the grass around him, leaving him none. At worst, they would butt him and push him around. So the shepherd prepared a "table" for the sick sheep.

The shepherd marked out an area about 20 ft (7 meters) x 15 ft (5 meters). He put his rod on one side and his staff on the other side. He lay down at the top of the protective rectangle, after he had placed his cloak at the bottom. No other sheep dared to cross over the rod, staff, cloak or shepherd to eat any of the grass.

In the presence of his enemies the ill sheep now had a "table" to protect him.

Psalms to turn to in a time of crisis

Psalms 4; 5; 11; 28; 41; 55; 59; 64; 70; 109; 120; 140; 141; 142.

Psalms for times of joy

Joy in the Psalms

Over the next month, select one verse about joy from the Psalms and take it with you through your day.

1. Joy and the heart	"You have filled my heart with greater joy ..." *(See also Psalms 19:8; 28:7; 97:11; 119:111.)*	*Psalm 4:7*
2. Joy and shouting and singing praises	"Let them ever sing for joy." *(See also Psalms 20:5; 27:6; 33:3; 35:27; 42:4; 47:1, 5; 65:8, 13; 66:1; 67:4; 71:23; 81:1; 89:12; 92:4; 95:1; 96:12; 98:4, 6, 8; 10:43; 107:22; 118:15; 126:2, 5, 6; 132:9, 16; 137:3; 149:5.)*	*Psalm 5:11.*
3. Joy in God's presence	"You will fill me with joy in your presence." *(See also Psalm 21:6.)*	*Psalm 16:11*
4. Joy linked to delight and gladness	"... to God, my joy and my delight." *(See also Psalms 45:15; 51:8; 90:14.)*	*Psalm 43:4*
5. Filled with joy	"We are filled with joy."	*Psalm 126:3*
6. Joy and salvation	"Restore to me the joy of your salvation."	*Psalm 51:12*
7. Clothed with joy	"... clothed me with joy."	*Psalm 30:11*
8. Anointed with joy	"God, your God, has set you above your companions by anointing you with the oil of joy."	*Psalm 45:7*
9. Comfort and joy	"When anxiety was great within me, your consolation brought joy to my soul."	*Psalm 94:19*

Psalm 100

Shout for joy to the Lord, all the earth.
Worship the Lord with gladness;
   come before him with joyful songs.
Know that the Lord is God.
   It is he who made us, and we are his;
   we are his people, the sheep of his
   pasture.
Enter his gates with thanksgiving
   and his courts with praise;
   give thanks to him and praise his name.
For the Lord is good and his love endures
   for ever;
   his faithfulness continues through all
   generations.
Psalm 100:1-5

Hallelujah Psalms

These psalms use the term Hallelujah,
meaning "Praise Jah (Jehovah)".

   Psalms 115; 116; 117; 146; 147; 148;
149; 150.

A PRAYER TO PRAY

LORD, MAKE ME AN INSTRUMENT OF YOUR PEACE.
WHERE THERE IS HATRED, LET ME SOW LOVE,
WHERE THERE IS INJURY, PARDON,
WHERE THERE IS DOUBT, FAITH,
WHERE THERE IS DARKNESS, LIGHT,
WHERE THERE IS SADNESS, JOY.

O DIVINE MASTER, GRANT THAT I MAY NOT SO MUCH
     SEEK TO BE CONSOLED AS TO CONSOLE,
NOT SO MUCH TO BE UNDERSTOOD AS TO
UNDERSTAND,
NOT SO MUCH TO BE LOVED AS TO LOVE;
FOR IT IS IN GIVING THAT WE RECEIVE,
IT IS IN PARDONING THAT WE ARE PARDONED,
IT IS IN DYING THAT WE ARE BORN TO ETERNAL LIFE.

Traditionally attributed to Francis of Assisi

Psalms for times of dryness

Spiritual dryness and the Christian

It is true that unconfessed sin can and does cause much disturbance in a Christian's walk with Jesus.

A SAYING ABOUT PRAYER

"SEVEN DAYS WITHOUT PRAYER MAKES ONE WEAK."

> "If I had cherished sin in my heart, the Lord would not have listened [to my prayers]." *Psalm 66:18*

It is not true that all spiritual dryness can be put down to unconfessed sin.

Psalms 42 and 43

When you are down, read Psalms 42 and 43.
Write down in a notebook what lessons God teaches you as you read slowly through them for a second time.

Lessons from Psalms 42 and 43

Lesson number one: Tell God what you feel like

1. The Psalmist admitted his own feelings. He talks about being "downcast" in *Psalm 42:5-6, 11; 43:5*	"My soul is downcast within me." *Psalm 42:5*
2. The Psalmist does not beat about the bush. He describes specific troubles and symptoms. Godly people can easily feel low when attacked by unbelievers.	"My bones suffer mortal agony as my foes taunt me, saying to me all day long, 'Where is your God?'" *Psalm 42:10*
3. The Psalmist tells God that he feels that the Lord has forsaken and forgotten him.	"Why have you forgotten me?" *Psalm 42:9* "Why have you rejected me?" *Psalm 43:2*

Lesson number two: Remember who God is

1. The Psalmist calls God his Rock.	"I say to God my Rock." *Psalm 42:9*
2. God can give the Psalmist light and truth.	"Send forth your light and your truth, let them guide me." *Psalm 43:3*
3. The Psalmist remembers that God is his stronghold.	"You God are my stronghold." *Psalm 43:2*
4. God is the Psalmist's Savior.	"... my Savior and my God." *Psalm 42:11; 43:5*

Lesson number three: Put your trust in God

The Psalmist gives himself a good talking to and concludes that he must trust God.	"Put your hope in God, for I will yet praise him, my Savior and my God." *Psalm 42:11; 43:5*

Psalms for times of sin

Psalm 51

This psalm is thought to have been written after David had committed adultery with Bathsheba, and in an attempt to cover this up arranged for Bathsheba's husband, Uriah, to be killed in battle. *See 2 Samuel 11.*

How could an adulterer and murderer continue to serve God? Only because he prayed Psalm 51 from his heart.

Read through the psalm for yourself and see how each verse has a positive message for a repentant sinner.

Have mercy on me, O God

Verse

1 Have mercy on me, O God, according to your unfailing love; according to your great compassion blot out my transgressions.
2 Wash away all my iniquity and cleanse me from my sin.
3 For I know my transgressions, and my sin is always before me.
4 Against you, you only, have I sinned and done what is evil in your sight, so that you are proved right when you speak and justified when you judge.
5 Surely I was sinful at birth, sinful from the time my mother conceived me.
6 Surely you desire truth in the inner parts; you teach me wisdom in the inmost place.
7 Cleanse me with hyssop, and I will be clean; wash me, and I will be whiter than snow.
8 Let me hear joy and gladness; let the bones you have crushed rejoice.
9 Hide your face from my sins and blot out all my iniquity.
10 Create in me a pure heart, O God, and renew a steadfast spirit within me.
11 Do not cast me from your presence or take your Holy Spirit from me.
12 Restore to me the joy of your salvation and grant me a willing spirit, to sustain me.
13 Then I will teach transgressors your ways, and sinners will turn back to you.
14 Save me from bloodguilt, O God, the God who saves me, and my tongue will sing of your righteousness.
15 O Lord, open my lips, and my mouth will declare your praise.
16 You do not delight in sacrifice, or I would bring it; you do not take pleasure in burnt offerings.

17 The sacrifices of God are a broken spirit; a broken and contrite heart, O God, you will not despise.

18 In your good pleasure make Zion prosper; build up the walls of Jerusalem.

19 Then there will be righteous sacrifices, whole burnt offerings to delight you; then bulls will be offered on your altar.

Psalm 51

What kind of prayers does God answer?
Prayers that come from:

1. An obedient heart	"… we receive from him [God] anything we ask, because we obey his commands."	*1 John 3:22*
2. A forgiving heart	"And when you stand praying, if you hold anything against anyone, forgive him, so that your Father in heaven may forgive you your sins."	*Mark 11:25*
3. A heart that does not doubt	"But when he asks, he must believe and not doubt, because he who doubts is like a wave of the sea, blown and tossed by the wind."	*James 1:6*
4. A broken heart	"A broken and contrite heart, O God, you will not despise."	*Psalm 51:17*
5. An undivided heart	"You will seek me and find me when you seek me with all your heart."	*Jeremiah 29:13*
6. A prayerful heart	"If you remain in me and my words remain in you, ask whatever you wish, and it will be given you."	*John 15:7*
7. A heart taught by	"The Spirit helps us in our weakness. We do not know what we ought to pray for, but the Spirit himself intercedes for us with groans that words cannot express."	*Romans 8:26*

Psalms

Psalms which breathe deep sorrow for sin:
Psalms 6; 25; 32; 38; 39; 40; 51; 102; 130.

Jesus at prayer

Jesus often prayed

"Jesus *often* withdrew to lonely places and prayed." *Luke 5:16*

Matthew, Mark, Luke and John record fifteen occasions when Jesus prayed. The writer to the Hebrews adds,

> "During the days of Jesus' life on earth, he offered up prayers and petitions with loud cries and tears to the one who could save him from death, and he was heard because of his reverent submission." *Hebrews 5:7*

Jesus is our model

There are many ways in which we can imitate Jesus in his praying.

1. Jesus praised God

"At that time Jesus, full of joy through the Holy Spirit, said, 'I praise you Father, Lord of heaven and earth, because you have hidden these things from the wise and learned, and revealed them to little children.'" *Luke 10:21*

2. Jesus gave thanks to God

Before feeding the 5,000, Jesus asked God to bless the five loaves and two fish.

"Taking the five loaves and the two fish and looking up to heaven, he gave thanks and broke the loaves." *Mark 6:41*

3. Jesus asked for things in his prayers

In his moment of great distress Jesus prayed to his heavenly Father.

"On reaching the place, he said to them, 'Pray that you will not fall into temptation.'

He withdrew about a stone's throw beyond them, knelt down and prayed, 'Father, if you are willing, take this cup from me; yet not my will, but yours be done.'

An angel from heaven appeared to him and strengthened him.

And being in anguish, he prayed more earnestly, and his sweat was like drops of blood falling to the ground." *Luke 22:40-44*

4. Jesus prayed for other people

"When they came to the place of the Skull, there they crucified him, along with the criminals – one on his right, the other on his left. Jesus said, 'Father, forgive them, for they do not know what they are doing.'" *Luke 23:34*

Jesus prayed at critical times in his life

1. At his baptism

"When all the people were being baptized, Jesus was baptized too. And as he was praying, heaven was opened and the Holy Spirit descended on him in bodily form like a dove." *Luke 3:21-22*

2. Before he chose his twelve disciples

"One of those days Jesus went out to a mountainside to pray, and spent the night praying to God. When morning came, he called his disciples to him and chose twelve of them." *Luke 6:13*

3. In face of temptation

After the miracle of the feeding of the five thousand the people tried to make Jesus their king. This was a temptation to avoid the cross and Jesus overcame this temptation by seeking refuge in prayer.

"After the people saw the miraculous sign that Jesus did, they began to say, 'Surely this is the Prophet who is to come into the world.' Jesus, knowing that they intended to come and make him king by force, withdrew again to a mountain by himself." *John 6:14-15*

4. From the cross

"Jesus called out with a loud voice, 'Father, into your hands I commit my spirit.'" *Luke 23:46*

"Jesus said, 'It is finished.' With that he bowed his head and gave up his spirit." *John 19:30*

55

Praying for others

The prophet Samuel and prayer
Prayer dominated Samuel's life, from start to finish.

1. He was born in answer to prayer.	*See 1 Samuel 1:10-28*
2. His name means *asked of God.*	*See 1 Samuel 1:20*
3. Deliverance at Mispah came	*See 1 Samuel 7:2-13*
4. When Israel asked for a king, Samuel prayed.	*See 1 Samuel 8:6, 21*
5. He prayed for his people all the time.	"As for me, far be it from me that I should sin against the Lord by failing to pray for you." *1 Samuel 12:23*

Samuel thought that it was sinful not to pray for God's people.

What about keeping a prayer list?
On one page you could have *Prayers for Every Day.* This might include your closest family and friends.

The next seven pages could be for each day of the week. By adding people's names and things to pray for on these days it would ensure that you pray for them once a week.

You could also use the next thirty-one pages to pray for different people and things once a month.

Is it wrong or selfish to bother God with trifling things?
Parents long for their children to tell them about all the joys and difficulties of their days. And God loves us much more than any parent can.

"... in everything, by prayer and petition with thanksgiving, present your requests to God." *Philippians 4:6*

Praying for your friends, children and spiritual children

What should you pray for when you pray for your friends? Christians are spiritual parents to those they lead to Christ and to those they are spiritually responsible for. They will pray for the same things that Christian parents pray for their children.

1. That they will know Jesus as their Savior.

2. That they will be protected from Satan in all areas of their lives: spiritual, emotional and physical. Pray as Jesus did. "My prayer is not that you will take them out of the world but that you protect them from the evil one." *John 17:15*

3. That they will have good friends, desire the right kind of friends and be protected from the wrong kind of friends. "My son, if sinners entice you, do not give in to them. If they say 'Come along with us; let's lie in wait for someone's blood, let's waylay some harmless soul.'" *Proverbs 1:10-11*

4. That they will serve Jesus Christ wholeheartedly. "Therefore, I urge you, brothers, in view of God's mercy, to offer your bodies as living sacrifices, holy and pleasing to God – which is your spiritual worship. Do not conform any longer to the pattern of this world, but be transformed by the renewing of your mind. Then you will be able to test and approve what God's will is – his good, pleasing and perfect will." *Romans 12:1-2*

When we pray are we asking God to change his mind?

There are many things about prayer that are a mystery. But it seems that God, in his love, calls us to be his partners in his work in this world.

"For we are God's fellow-workers." *1 Corinthians 3:9*

Jesus commands us to pray. *See Luke 10:2*
We are promised that our prayers are effective. *See James 5:16*

Keeping a prayer diary

A prayer diary of journal
This is different from a prayer list which is just a list of people and things to pray for.

A prayer diary is a record of how you have found that God has answered your prayers. By recording how God has answered a request, you will be encouraged to keep praying.

Making a prayer diary
In a notebook draw four columns down the page.

Column 1	Column 2	Column 3	Column 4
Date of prayer request	Prayer request	How prayer was answered	Date of answered prayer

Then fill in a line with the details of the most important thing you are praying about this week.

You can add to it as much as you like. One topic per week is manageable for most people.

When a prayer request is answered that is the cue for giving thanks to God.

Praying for people to be converted

"I spent the evening praying incessantly for divine assistance and that I might not be self-dependent. What I passed through was remarkable, and there appeared to be nothing of any importance to me but holiness of heart and life, and the conversion of the heathen to God. I cared not where or how I lived, or what hardships I went through so that I could but gain souls to Christ."
David Brainerd, Diary, 21 July 1744

So why does so much prayer seem to be unanswered?

We have such wonderful promises about prayer in the Bible from Jesus.

"If you believe, you will receive whatever you ask for in prayer."
Matthew 21:22

1. Being out of tune with God and His word	"If you remain in me and my words remain in you, ask whatever you wish, and it will be given you."	*John 15:7*
2. Lack of desire to please Jesus	"We ... receive from him anything we ask, because we obey his commands and do what pleases him."	*1 John 3:22*
3. Unconfessed sin	"The face of the Lord is against those who do evil."	*1 Peter 3:12*
4. Having the wrong motives	"When you ask, you do not receive, because you ask with wrong motives, that you may spend what you get on your pleasures."	*James 4:3*
5. Praying with lack of faith	"Without faith it is impossible to please God."	*Hebrews 11:6*
6. Lack of perseverance	"Then Jesus told his disciples a parable to show them that they should always pray and not give up."	*Luke 18:1*

Paul's prayers

Paul's prayers for the first Christian churches

Paul's thirteen letters in the New Testament were not just filled with giving instructions but they record the prayers he prayed for the different churches.

Paul's prayer for the Ephesians

"For this reason I kneel before the Father, from whom his whole family in heaven and on earth derives its name. I pray that out of his glorious riches he may strengthen you with power through his Spirit in your inner being, so that Christ may dwell in your hearts through faith. And I pray that you, being rooted and established in love, may have power, together with all the saints, to grasp how wide and long and high and deep is the love of Christ, and to know this love that surpasses knowledge – that you may be filled to the measure of all the fullness of God."
Ephesians 3:14-19

Church written to
1. The Ephesians
2. The Philippians
3. The Colossians
4. The Thessalonians

Pray Bible prayers

One way to pray for people is to select a prayer in the Bible, such as Ephesians 3:14-19, and use it as a basis of prayer, praying the prayer that Paul prayed for the Ephesian Christians – inserting the name of someone you are concerned for today.

Romans 16

Paul prayed for people by name. Have you ever read through Romans 16 and thought it consisted of just a long list of names? Read through this list of over two dozen people and see what Paul prayed for as he mentioned each person by name.

Theme of prayer	Extract from prayer	
Enlightenment	"That you may know the hope to which he has called you."	*Ephesians 1:18 (See Ephesians 1:15-19)*
Perseverence	"He who began a good work in you will carry it on to completion until the day of Christ Jesus."	*Philippians 1:6*
God's will	"... asking God to fill you with the knowledge of his will through all spiritual wisdom and understanding."	*Colossians 1:9*
Thanksgiving for faith, love, and hope	"We continually remember before our God and Father your work produced by faith, your labor prompted by love, and your endurance inspired by hope in our Lord Jesus Christ."	*1 Thessalonians 1:2-3*

Should you pray for people you've never seen?

Here is Paul's prayer for a group of Christians he had never met.

"Since the day we heard about you, we have not stopped praying for you and asking God to fill you with the knowledge of his will."
Colossians 1:9

More Bible prayers

How James said we should pray
James 5:13-18

Verse

14 "Is any one of you sick? He should call the elders of the church to pray over him and anoint him with oil in the name of the Lord."

15 "And the prayer offered in faith will make the sick person well; the Lord will raise him up. If he has sinned, he will be forgiven."

16 "Therefore confess your sins to each other and pray for each other so that you may be healed. The prayer of a righteous man is powerful and effective."

17 "Elijah was a man just like us. He prayed earnestly that it would not rain, and it did not rain on the land for three and a half years."

1. Be united in prayer.	"Call the elders of the church to pray."	*Verse 14*
2. Believe as you pray.	"The prayer offered in faith."	*Verse 15*
3. Have your own sin dealt with before you pray.	"Confess your sins to each other."	*Verse 16*
4. Pray for others.	"Pray for each other."	*Verse 16*
5. Be definite as you pray.	"That it would not rain."	*Verse 17*

Making progress in prayer

One of the best ways to find help in praying is to turn to the prayers in the Bible and see what God teaches you about how other people prayed to God.

King Hezekiah's song of praise for healing

"A writing of Hezekiah king of Judah after his illness and recovery:

I said, 'In the prime of my life
    must I go through the gates of death
    and be robbed of the rest of my years?'
I said, 'I will not again see the Lord,
    the Lord, in the land of the living;
no longer will I look on mankind,
    or be with those who now dwell in this world.
... But what can I say?
    He has spoken to me, and he himself has done this.
I will walk humbly all my years
    because of this anguish of my soul.
Lord, by such things men live;
    and my spirit finds life in them too.
You restored me to health
    and let me live. ...
The living, the living – they praise you,
    as I am doing today;
fathers tell their children
    about your faithfulness.
Isaiah 38:9-11, 15-16, 19

Praising God
despite everything

Pray anyway

There are no times when we should not pray. But different kinds of prayers are appropriate to different situations.

> "Is any one of you in trouble? He should pray. Is anyone happy? Let him sing songs of praise."
> *James 5:13*

God's promised presence

> "The Lord our God is near us whenever we pray to him."
> *Deuteronomy 4:7*

So God is close to us when we pray, whether we feel him or not; whether we are on our own or with many other people. This is good to remember when we just don't feel like praying.

Disasters and prayer

The fall of Jerusalem and the destruction of the temple was the greatest disaster the Israelites suffered. Yet these words of hope and burning faith are found in the middle of the Book of Lamentations, a book which describes their devastating condition.

> "Because of the Lord's great love we
>   are not consumed,
>   for his compassions never fail.
> They are new every morning,
>   great is your faithfulness."
> *Lamentations 3:22-23*